Operation Zarb-e-Azb: The Pakistani Military Battle Against Militant Groups in North Waziristan

Copyright Page

TITLE: Operation Zarb-e-Azb: The Pakistani Military Battle Against Militant Groups in North Waziristan

1ST Edition

Copyright @ 2023

Roberto M. Rodriguez. All rights reserved.

ISBN: 9798223497479

Table of Contents

Operation Zarb-e-Azb: The Pakistani Military Battle Against Militant Groups in North Waziristan

By Roberto Miguel Rodriguez

Chapter 1: Operation Zarb-e-Azb: The 2014-2017 Pakistani Military Operation Against Militant Groups in North Waziristan

Background and Context of Operation Zarb-e-Azb

The subchapter titled "Background and Context of Operation Zarb-e-Azb" provides an in-depth understanding of the factors that led to the initiation of this significant Pakistani military operation against militant groups in North Waziristan. Military historians and individuals interested in Operation Zarb-e-Azb will find this subchapter particularly informative.

To comprehensively grasp the intricacies of Operation Zarb-e-Azb, it is crucial to delve into the historical background and contextual framework surrounding the operation. This subchapter aims to shed light on the factors that necessitated this military intervention.

The subchapter begins by exploring the rise of militant groups in North Waziristan and their increasing threat to regional and international security. It delves into the origins of these groups, their ideological underpinnings, and their objectives. The subchapter also examines the role of North Waziristan as a safe haven and launchpad for these militant groups, highlighting the challenges it posed to Pakistan's counter-terrorism efforts.

Furthermore, the subchapter analyzes the Pakistani government's response to this growing threat, emphasizing the need for a comprehensive military operation. It explores the decision-making process that led to the formulation and execution of Operation

Zarb-e-Azb. This includes a discussion on the involvement of intelligence agencies in planning and coordinating the operation.

In addition, the subchapter explores the role of international collaboration in Operation Zarb-e-Azb. It discusses the cooperation between Pakistan and its international allies, including the United States, in addressing the militant threat in North Waziristan. The subchapter also examines the impact of Operation Zarb-e-Azb on regional security dynamics, taking into account the concerns of neighboring countries and the broader implications for regional stability.

To provide a holistic understanding of the operation, the subchapter touches upon the humanitarian challenges and relief efforts during Operation Zarb-e-Azb. It highlights the impact of the military operation on the affected communities, both in terms of psychological and social consequences. It also discusses the role of media coverage and public perception of Operation Zarb-e-Azb in shaping public opinion and support for the operation.

Lastly, the subchapter concludes by analyzing the success and effectiveness of Operation Zarb-e-Azb in eliminating militant groups. It critically evaluates the achievements and shortcomings of the operation, drawing lessons for future counter-terrorism operations.

In summary, this subchapter provides a comprehensive overview of the background and context of Operation Zarb-e-Azb. It explores the historical origins of the militant threat in North Waziristan, the decision-making process leading to the operation, international collaboration, humanitarian challenges, and evaluates the operation's effectiveness. Military historians and those interested in Operation Zarb-e-Azb will find this subchapter to be an invaluable resource.

Objectives and Strategies of Operation Zarb-e-Azb

Introduction:

Operation Zarb-e-Azb, the 2014-2017 Pakistani military operation against militant groups in North Waziristan, was a significant milestone in the country's counter-terrorism efforts. This subchapter aims to provide military historians with a comprehensive understanding of the objectives and strategies employed during Operation Zarb-e-Azb.

Objectives:

The primary objective of Operation Zarb-e-Azb was to eliminate militant groups operating in North Waziristan and restore peace and stability in the region. The operation aimed to dismantle the infrastructure of these groups, disrupt their command and control, and degrade their operational capabilities. Additionally, the operation sought to regain control of territory held by militants and establish the writ of the state.

Strategies:

1. Comprehensive Military Offensive: Operation Zarb-e-Azb involved a full-scale military offensive against militant strongholds in North Waziristan. The operation employed a combination of ground and air assets to target militant hideouts, training camps, and communication networks. The use of precision airstrikes and ground forces ensured minimal collateral damage and civilian casualties.

2. Intelligence-Based Operations: Intelligence agencies played a crucial role in planning and executing Operation Zarb-e-Azb. Timely and accurate intelligence enabled the military to identify high-value targets and disrupt militant networks. Coordinated efforts among various intelligence agencies ensured the success of the operation.

3. International Collaboration: Operation Zarb-e-Azb benefited from international collaboration, particularly in terms of intelligence sharing and technical assistance. Cooperation with allied countries enhanced

the effectiveness of the operation by providing valuable insights and resources.

4. Humanitarian Challenges and Relief Efforts: Recognizing the humanitarian challenges posed by the operation, the military simultaneously conducted relief efforts. The provision of food, shelter, and medical assistance to displaced civilians demonstrated a commitment to alleviate their suffering and garner public support.

5. Psychological and Social Consequences: Operation Zarb-e-Azb had significant psychological and social consequences on the affected communities. The military conducted psychological rehabilitation and social reintegration programs to address the trauma and ensure a smooth transition to normalcy.

Conclusion:

Operation Zarb-e-Azb successfully achieved its objectives by targeting and eliminating militant groups in North Waziristan. The comprehensive military offensive, intelligence-based operations, international collaboration, and humanitarian efforts were instrumental in its success. However, the operation also had psychological and social consequences that required rehabilitation and reintegration efforts. The lessons learned from Operation Zarb-e-Azb will serve as valuable insights for future counter-terrorism operations, further enhancing Pakistan's ability to combat militant groups effectively.

Planning and Execution of Operation Zarb-e-Azb

Operation Zarb-e-Azb, the 2014-2017 Pakistani military operation against militant groups in North Waziristan, was a decisive moment in the country's battle against terrorism. The successful execution of this operation not only had a profound impact on counter-terrorism efforts in Pakistan but also influenced regional security dynamics. The planning and execution of Operation Zarb-e-Azb involved meticulous strategies and coordination among various stakeholders.

The operation was meticulously planned by the Pakistani military, taking into account the complex terrain and the presence of entrenched militant groups. Intelligence agencies played a crucial role in gathering accurate information, identifying key targets, and neutralizing high-value targets. The collaboration between the military and intelligence agencies was instrumental in the success of the operation.

International collaboration also played a significant role in Operation Zarb-e-Azb. Pakistan received support from its international partners, including the United States, who provided intelligence sharing, training, and logistical support. This collaboration enhanced the capabilities of the Pakistani military and ensured a more coordinated and effective operation.

Operation Zarb-e-Azb not only focused on eliminating militant groups but also addressed humanitarian challenges and relief efforts. The operation was conducted with utmost consideration for the welfare of the affected communities. Efforts were made to minimize collateral damage and ensure the provision of humanitarian aid to the displaced population.

However, the psychological and social consequences of Operation Zarb-e-Azb on the affected communities cannot be overlooked. The operation disrupted the lives of many and caused displacement, trauma, and social upheaval. Efforts were made to mitigate these consequences through the provision of psychological support and rehabilitation programs.

The success and effectiveness of Operation Zarb-e-Azb in eliminating militant groups were undeniable. The operation significantly weakened and eliminated several prominent militant groups, disrupting their networks and reducing their ability to carry out attacks. The operation also had a positive impact on regional security dynamics by curbing cross-border terrorism and promoting stability in the region.

Media coverage and public perception of Operation Zarb-e-Azb in Pakistan played a crucial role in shaping public opinion. The media played a vital role in disseminating information and raising awareness about the objectives and progress of the operation. Public support and trust in the military's efforts were crucial for the success of the operation.

The role of drone strikes in supporting Operation Zarb-e-Azb cannot be ignored. These strikes targeted key militant leaders and disrupted their command structures. The precision and effectiveness of these strikes played a significant role in complementing the ground operation.

Operation Zarb-e-Azb provided valuable lessons for future counter-terrorism operations. The operation highlighted the importance of intelligence sharing, international collaboration, and the need for a comprehensive approach that addresses humanitarian challenges and social consequences. These lessons can inform and guide future counter-terrorism efforts, both in Pakistan and globally.

In conclusion, Operation Zarb-e-Azb was a landmark military operation that had far-reaching implications for Pakistan's battle against terrorism. The planning and execution of this operation involved meticulous strategies, international collaboration, and a focus on addressing humanitarian challenges. The operation's success in eliminating militant groups, its impact on regional security dynamics, and the lessons learned make it a significant case study for military historians and those interested in counter-terrorism efforts.

Role of Pakistani Armed Forces in Operation Zarb-e-Azb

The military historians will find the role of Pakistani Armed Forces in Operation Zarb-e-Azb to be of great significance in understanding the dynamics of counter-terrorism efforts in Pakistan. This subchapter aims to provide a comprehensive overview of the contributions made by the Pakistani Armed Forces during this operation.

Operation Zarb-e-Azb, which lasted from 2014 to 2017, was a major military offensive launched by the Pakistani Armed Forces against militant groups in North Waziristan. The objective was to eliminate the sanctuaries and infrastructure of these groups, which had posed a serious threat to national security.

The Pakistani Armed Forces played a vital role in planning and executing the operation. They conducted extensive intelligence gathering, which allowed them to identify and target key militant hideouts. The operation involved a combination of ground offensives, air strikes, and precise military operations to minimize civilian casualties.

The Pakistani Armed Forces displayed exemplary professionalism and courage throughout the operation. The soldiers faced intense counterattacks from well-armed and well-trained militants, yet they remained steadfast in their mission. Their commitment to the cause and dedication to the eradication of militancy in the region were commendable.

Furthermore, the Pakistani Armed Forces also collaborated with international partners during Operation Zarb-e-Azb. This collaboration included intelligence sharing, joint training exercises, and logistical support. The international community recognized the importance of this operation and extended their support to Pakistan in its fight against terrorism.

The success and effectiveness of Operation Zarb-e-Azb can be measured by the significant reduction in militant activities in North Waziristan. The operation resulted in the elimination of numerous militant leaders and their networks. It also disrupted the flow of weapons and funding to these groups, severely crippling their capabilities.

However, Operation Zarb-e-Azb also had psychological and social consequences on the affected communities. The displacement of thousands of people and the destruction of infrastructure created humanitarian challenges. The Pakistani Armed Forces, in collaboration with humanitarian organizations, worked tirelessly to provide relief and rehabilitation to the affected population.

In conclusion, the role of the Pakistani Armed Forces in Operation Zarb-e-Azb was pivotal in eliminating militant groups from North Waziristan. Their professionalism, courage, and collaboration with international partners played a crucial role in the success of this operation. However, it is important to acknowledge the humanitarian challenges and social consequences that arose as a result of the operation. The lessons learned from Operation Zarb-e-Azb will undoubtedly shape future counter-terrorism operations in Pakistan and serve as a valuable reference for military historians.

Key Military Leaders and Their Contributions to Operation Zarb-e-Azb

The success of any military operation is heavily dependent on the leadership and strategic decisions made by key military leaders. Operation Zarb-e-Azb, the Pakistani military's battle against militant groups in North Waziristan, was no exception. This subchapter aims to shed light on the contributions of these key military leaders and their significant role in the success of the operation.

General Raheel Sharif, the Chief of Army Staff during the operation, played a pivotal role in planning and executing Operation Zarb-e-Azb. His leadership and determination were instrumental in mobilizing the military and coordinating efforts between various branches. Under his command, the military launched a comprehensive offensive against the militants, targeting their hideouts, training camps, and communication networks.

Lieutenant General Asim Bajwa, the Director-General of the Inter-Services Public Relations, played a crucial role in shaping public perception and managing media coverage of the operation. His effective communication strategy ensured that the true objectives and progress of Operation Zarb-e-Azb were accurately portrayed to both domestic and international audiences.

Major General Sajjad Ghani, the Commander of the Special Services Group (SSG), led the elite commando force during the operation. The SSG, known for their exceptional combat skills, played a vital role in conducting high-risk operations, including clearing out heavily fortified militant positions and rescuing hostages.

Brigadier General Zahid Mehmood, the Commander of the 7th Infantry Division, led ground troops in the rugged terrain of North Waziristan. His strategic planning and coordination with air support units were crucial in ensuring the success of ground operations.

Air Marshal Sohail Aman, the Chief of Air Staff, provided vital air support to ground forces during Operation Zarb-e-Azb. The Pakistan Air Force carried out precision airstrikes, targeting militant strongholds and disrupting their supply lines. Air Marshal Aman's leadership and effective use of air power significantly contributed to the progress of the operation.

These key military leaders, along with their dedicated teams, worked tirelessly to eliminate militant groups and restore peace in North Waziristan. Their contributions, ranging from strategic planning to ground operations and air support, were essential in the success of Operation Zarb-e-Azb. The achievements of these military leaders serve as a testament to the effectiveness of their leadership and the Pakistani military's commitment to counter-terrorism efforts.

Chapter 2: Impact of Operation Zarb-e-Azb on Counter-terrorism Efforts in Pakistan

Reduction of Militant Attacks and Casualties

One of the key objectives of Operation Zarb-e-Azb was to significantly reduce militant attacks and casualties in North Waziristan, and this subchapter aims to evaluate the success of the operation in achieving this goal. By analyzing the data and statistics available, military historians can gain insights into the effectiveness of the Pakistani military's battle against militant groups in the region.

Operation Zarb-e-Azb was a comprehensive military operation launched in June 2014 to eliminate the menace of terrorism from North Waziristan. The region had long been a safe haven for various militant groups, including the Tehrik-i-Taliban Pakistan (TTP), Haqqani Network, and foreign fighters. These groups not only posed a threat to national security but also carried out devastating attacks across Pakistan.

One of the primary indicators of success in reducing militant attacks and casualties is the decline in overall security incidents. Throughout the operation, the Pakistani military launched targeted airstrikes, ground offensives, and house-to-house searches to flush out militants. These operations resulted in a significant decrease in the number of militant attacks, including suicide bombings and armed assaults, in North Waziristan.

Moreover, the operation also led to the dismantlement of terrorist infrastructure, including training camps, ammunition dumps, and communication networks. This disruption severely limited the militants' ability to plan and carry out attacks, further contributing to the reduction in violence and casualties.

In addition to the decline in security incidents, another measure of success is the decrease in civilian and military casualties. Operation Zarb-e-Azb placed a strong emphasis on minimizing collateral damage and protecting civilian lives. The military employed precise targeting techniques and intelligence-based operations to minimize civilian casualties.

Furthermore, the operation also focused on enhancing intelligence capabilities and strengthening border controls to prevent the infiltration of militants from neighboring Afghanistan. By targeting the leadership of militant groups and disrupting their support networks, the operation dealt a severe blow to these organizations, significantly reducing their capacity to launch attacks.

In conclusion, Operation Zarb-e-Azb successfully achieved its objective of reducing militant attacks and casualties in North Waziristan. Through targeted operations, disruption of terrorist infrastructure, and enhanced intelligence capabilities, the Pakistani military significantly weakened militant groups operating in the region. The decline in security incidents and civilian casualties is a testament to the effectiveness of this operation in combating terrorism. However, it is important for military historians to continue studying the long-term impact of Operation Zarb-e-Azb on counter-terrorism efforts in Pakistan and draw lessons for future operations in the fight against militant groups.

Disruption of Militant Networks and Infrastructure

Disrupting militant networks and infrastructure was a critical objective of Operation Zarb-e-Azb, the Pakistani military's battle against militant groups in North Waziristan from 2014 to 2017. This subchapter explores the strategies and tactics employed to dismantle these networks and undermine their capacity to carry out acts of terrorism.

The operation aimed to sever the lifelines of militant groups by targeting their command and control centers, training camps, communication networks, and financial resources. The Pakistani military, in collaboration with intelligence agencies, meticulously planned and executed precision strikes to degrade the infrastructure that supported these networks. Through a combination of ground operations and aerial bombardment, the military targeted key locations such as hideouts, weapon caches, and ammunition factories, rendering them inoperable.

One of the primary methods used to disrupt the militants' networks was the targeting of their leadership. By eliminating key figures within the militant groups, the Pakistani military aimed to decapitate their command structure and create a leadership vacuum. This tactic not only disrupted their ability to coordinate attacks but also sowed internal divisions and weakened their overall effectiveness.

Additionally, Operation Zarb-e-Azb focused on severing the militants' communication networks. By targeting their radio stations, satellite phones, and internet facilities, the military aimed to disrupt their ability to coordinate and disseminate propaganda. This tactic not only hindered their operational capabilities but also undermined their ability to recruit new members and garner support.

Another crucial aspect of disrupting militant networks was targeting their financial resources. The Pakistani military, in collaboration with intelligence agencies and financial institutions, identified and froze the assets of individuals and organizations involved in financing terrorism. By cutting off their funding sources, the military aimed to undermine their ability to carry out attacks and sustain their operations.

Through the disruption of militant networks and infrastructure, Operation Zarb-e-Azb significantly hampered the operational capabilities of militant groups in North Waziristan. This subchapter delves into the specific strategies and tactics employed to achieve this objective and evaluates the success and effectiveness of these measures.

Military historians and those interested in the impact of counter-terrorism efforts in Pakistan will find this subchapter particularly insightful. It provides a comprehensive analysis of the methods used to disrupt militant networks and infrastructure, shedding light on the lessons learned from Operation Zarb-e-Azb for future counter-terrorism operations.

Rehabilitation and Reintegration of Former Militants

One of the crucial aspects of any military operation against militant groups is not just eliminating their presence but also addressing the root causes that lead individuals to join these groups in the first place. This subchapter focuses on the rehabilitation and reintegration efforts carried out by the Pakistani military as part of Operation Zarb-e-Azb in North Waziristan.

Understanding that military force alone cannot solve the problem of militancy, the Pakistani military recognized the need for a comprehensive approach that would help former militants reintegrate into society and prevent them from returning to their previous activities. This involved addressing various aspects such as ideological reorientation, skill development, and providing psychological and social support.

One of the key programs implemented under Operation Zarb-e-Azb was the establishment of deradicalization centers. These centers aimed to challenge the extremist ideologies that had influenced the militants and promote a more moderate interpretation of Islam. Trained counselors and religious scholars engaged with the former militants, providing them with alternative perspectives and helping them develop a more tolerant worldview.

In addition to ideological reorientation, the rehabilitation process also focused on equipping the former militants with vocational skills. Through various training programs, they were given the opportunity to learn practical skills such as carpentry, welding, and agriculture. By providing them with viable employment options, the military aimed to ensure that these individuals had a sustainable means of livelihood and were less likely to be drawn back into militancy.

Furthermore, recognizing the psychological trauma that many former militants had experienced, Operation Zarb-e-Azb also included counseling and therapy services. These services aimed to address the mental health issues faced by the individuals and provide them with the necessary support to overcome their past experiences.

The success and effectiveness of the rehabilitation and reintegration efforts carried out under Operation Zarb-e-Azb can be measured by the number of individuals who have successfully reintegrated into society and remained non-engaged in militant activities. These efforts not only contribute to the long-term stability of the region but also serve as a model for future counter-terrorism operations.

Overall, the rehabilitation and reintegration of former militants is a critical component of any military operation against militant groups. By addressing the root causes and providing comprehensive support, Operation Zarb-e-Azb has made significant strides in rehabilitating individuals and preventing them from returning to militancy.

Strengthening of Law Enforcement and Intelligence Agencies

The success of any military operation heavily relies on the coordination and effectiveness of law enforcement and intelligence agencies. In the case of Operation Zarb-e-Azb, the Pakistani military's battle against militant groups in North Waziristan, the strengthening of these agencies played a crucial role in achieving the operation's objectives.

Law enforcement agencies, such as the police and paramilitary forces, were instrumental in maintaining law and order in the areas cleared during the operation. They were responsible for preventing the re-emergence of militant groups and ensuring the safety and security of the local population. The deployment of additional personnel, along with enhanced training and equipment, allowed these agencies to effectively carry out their duties.

Intelligence agencies, on the other hand, played a pivotal role in gathering and analyzing information about militant groups and their activities. The intelligence gathered not only helped in identifying high-value targets but also in planning and executing precise operations. The collaboration between different intelligence agencies, both domestic and international, further strengthened the intelligence network and facilitated the sharing of vital information.

To strengthen these agencies, several measures were taken during and after Operation Zarb-e-Azb. First and foremost, there was an increased focus on training and capacity building. Specialized training programs were designed to equip law enforcement and intelligence personnel with the necessary skills and knowledge to tackle the evolving threat of terrorism.

Furthermore, efforts were made to enhance the technological capabilities of these agencies. The introduction of modern surveillance systems, communication equipment, and intelligence-sharing platforms improved their operational efficiency. Close coordination between the military and these agencies also ensured effective collaboration in planning and executing counter-terrorism operations.

The strengthening of law enforcement and intelligence agencies not only contributed to the success of Operation Zarb-e-Azb but also had a lasting impact on counter-terrorism efforts in Pakistan. The improved capabilities and coordination of these agencies have helped in preventing the resurgence of militant groups in the region. Additionally, the lessons learned from this operation have provided valuable insights for future counter-terrorism operations, both domestically and internationally.

In conclusion, the strengthening of law enforcement and intelligence agencies played a crucial role in the success of Operation Zarb-e-Azb. Through enhanced training, capacity building, and technological advancements, these agencies were able to effectively tackle the threat posed by militant groups. The lessons learned from this operation have not only improved counter-terrorism efforts in Pakistan but also serve as a valuable resource for future operations.

Challenges and Limitations in Sustaining the Success of Operation Zarb-e-Azb

As military historians delve into the details of Operation Zarb-e-Azb, it becomes evident that while the operation achieved significant success in eliminating militant groups in North Waziristan, it also faced several challenges and limitations in sustaining that success. These challenges, although not insurmountable, shed light on the complexities of counter-terrorism efforts in a region plagued by extremism and violence.

One of the foremost challenges was the porous border between Pakistan and Afghanistan. Despite efforts to secure the border, militants often found safe havens across the border, allowing them to regroup and launch attacks. This cross-border movement posed a significant challenge in sustaining the gains made during Operation Zarb-e-Azb and highlighted the need for enhanced collaboration with Afghan authorities.

Another limitation was the issue of internally displaced persons (IDPs). The operation resulted in a massive displacement of the local population, creating a humanitarian crisis. Providing relief efforts and ensuring the safe return and rehabilitation of the IDPs proved to be a major challenge for the Pakistani military and the government. The long-term consequences of this displacement, including the psychological and social impact on the affected communities, cannot be overlooked.

Furthermore, sustaining the success of Operation Zarb-e-Azb required continued intelligence gathering and effective coordination among various security agencies. The role of intelligence agencies in planning and executing the operation was crucial, and any lapse in intelligence gathering could have undermined the gains made. Therefore, it was imperative to maintain the momentum and ensure ongoing collaboration between intelligence agencies.

Media coverage and public perception also played a significant role in sustaining the success of Operation Zarb-e-Azb. While the operation received considerable media coverage, it was essential to maintain public support and debunk any misinformation or negative narratives. The military needed to effectively communicate the objectives and achievements of the operation to shape public opinion and counter any backlash.

Lastly, the sustainability of Operation Zarb-e-Azb required a comprehensive approach to address the root causes of militancy and extremism. Merely eliminating militant groups through military force was not sufficient. There was a need for long-term strategies, including socio-economic development, education, and countering extremist ideologies, to prevent the resurgence of militancy in the region.

In conclusion, Operation Zarb-e-Azb faced several challenges and limitations in sustaining its success. Addressing these challenges required enhanced collaboration with Afghanistan, effective relief efforts for the IDPs, continued intelligence gathering, positive media coverage, and comprehensive long-term strategies. By analyzing these challenges and limitations, military historians can derive valuable lessons for future counter-terrorism operations, ensuring a more holistic and sustainable approach to combating terrorism.

Chapter 3: The Role of International Collaboration in Operation Zarb-e-Azb

Collaboration with United States and NATO Allies

The success of any military operation is greatly influenced by the level of collaboration and cooperation between different nations and their armed forces. This subchapter explores the crucial role played by the United States and NATO allies in Operation Zarb-e-Azb, the Pakistani military's battle against militant groups in North Waziristan.

Recognizing the transnational nature of terrorism and the need for a united front against it, Pakistan actively sought assistance from its international partners, particularly the United States and NATO. This collaboration was imperative for several reasons. Firstly, it provided Pakistan with access to advanced intelligence capabilities, enabling them to gather crucial information about the locations and activities of militant groups operating in the region. This intelligence sharing played a pivotal role in planning and executing targeted military strikes, which were vital in eliminating these militant groups.

Additionally, the collaboration with the United States and NATO allies facilitated the provision of logistical support, training, and equipment to the Pakistani military. This support greatly enhanced the operational capabilities of the Pakistani forces, enabling them to effectively combat the well-armed and well-trained militant groups in North Waziristan.

Furthermore, the collaboration with international partners also helped in addressing the humanitarian challenges that arose during Operation Zarb-e-Azb. The United States and NATO allies provided significant assistance in relief efforts, ensuring the provision of food, shelter, and medical aid to the affected communities. This support not only alleviated the suffering of the local population but also helped in winning their hearts and minds, thus weakening the support base of the militant groups.

Collaboration with the United States and NATO allies also had a significant impact on the regional security dynamics. It sent a strong message to the neighboring countries that terrorism would not be tolerated, and that a united front would be formed to counter it. This collaboration fostered greater trust and cooperation among the regional powers, leading to improved security cooperation in the future.

In conclusion, the collaboration with the United States and NATO allies played a pivotal role in the success of Operation Zarb-e-Azb. It provided Pakistan with crucial intelligence, logistical support, and humanitarian assistance, while also strengthening regional security dynamics. This chapter will delve deeper into the specifics of this collaboration and its impact on the overall success of the operation. Military historians, as well as those interested in the various niches of Operation Zarb-e-Azb, will find this subchapter informative and insightful.

Support from Regional Powers and Intelligence Sharing

One of the key factors that contributed to the success of Operation Zarb-e-Azb, the Pakistani military's battle against militant groups in North Waziristan, was the support received from regional powers and intelligence sharing. This subchapter aims to shed light on the crucial role played by these factors in the operation's effectiveness.

Regional powers such as China, Iran, and Afghanistan played a significant role in supporting Operation Zarb-e-Azb. China, being a strategic ally of Pakistan, provided substantial political, economic, and military assistance. Their support helped strengthen Pakistan's resolve in combating terrorism and ensured the availability of necessary resources to carry out the operation effectively.

Intelligence sharing also played a pivotal role in the success of Operation Zarb-e-Azb. The sharing of vital intelligence with Pakistan by various regional powers and intelligence agencies proved instrumental in identifying militant hideouts, their networks, and their sources of funding. This information enabled the Pakistani military to plan and execute targeted operations, thereby significantly weakening the infrastructure of militant groups in the region.

The intelligence sharing network established during Operation Zarb-e-Azb not only included regional powers but also international intelligence agencies such as the CIA and MI6. The collaboration between these agencies and the Pakistani military was crucial in gathering actionable intelligence and conducting targeted operations against high-value targets. This collaboration also helped build trust and cooperation, which further strengthened the regional security dynamics.

The success of Operation Zarb-e-Azb in eliminating militant groups would not have been possible without the support and intelligence sharing from regional powers. The collective efforts of these countries and intelligence agencies ensured a coordinated approach in combating terrorism, preventing the escape of militants across borders, and disrupting their funding networks.

In conclusion, the support from regional powers and intelligence sharing were vital components in the success of Operation Zarb-e-Azb. The collaboration between Pakistan and various regional and international intelligence agencies not only enhanced the effectiveness of the operation but also strengthened regional security dynamics. The lessons learned from this collaboration can serve as a blueprint for future counter-terrorism operations, emphasizing the significance of regional cooperation and intelligence sharing in combating militant groups effectively.

International Aid and Assistance in Humanitarian Efforts

Throughout history, military operations have often been accompanied by humanitarian challenges and the need for international aid and assistance. Operation Zarb-e-Azb, the 2014-2017 Pakistani military operation against militant groups in North Waziristan, was no exception. In this subchapter, we will delve into the crucial role played by international collaboration and humanitarian relief efforts during this operation.

Operation Zarb-e-Azb was a significant milestone in Pakistan's counter-terrorism efforts. As the operation unfolded, it became evident that the humanitarian challenges were immense. The displaced population, consisting of hundreds of thousands of people, required urgent assistance. International aid organizations, such as the United Nations and various non-governmental organizations, stepped in to provide much-needed support.

The provision of humanitarian aid during Operation Zarb-e-Azb was a complex task. The military operation had created a massive displacement crisis, requiring the mobilization of resources on a large scale. International aid organizations worked closely with the Pakistani government and military to establish relief camps, provide food, clean water, healthcare, and other essential services to the affected population.

Cooperation between international aid organizations and the Pakistani military was crucial in ensuring the smooth delivery of humanitarian assistance. The military provided security and logistical support, enabling aid organizations to navigate the challenging terrain and reach remote areas. This collaboration was a testament to the importance of international partnerships in tackling complex humanitarian crises.

Additionally, international assistance played a vital role in addressing the psychological and social consequences of Operation Zarb-e-Azb on affected communities. Trauma counseling, rehabilitation programs, and community-based initiatives helped individuals and communities heal and rebuild their lives.

The success and effectiveness of Operation Zarb-e-Azb cannot be evaluated without considering the role of international aid and assistance. The collaboration between the Pakistani military and international partners ensured that the humanitarian needs of the affected population were met, minimizing the impact of the operation on innocent civilians.

Moreover, the international aid provided during Operation Zarb-e-Azb had broader implications for regional security dynamics. By addressing the humanitarian challenges, international partners contributed to stabilizing the region and preventing the resurgence of militant groups.

In conclusion, international aid and assistance played a pivotal role in addressing the humanitarian challenges during Operation Zarb-e-Azb. The collaboration between the Pakistani military and international partners facilitated the delivery of essential services to the displaced population. Furthermore, international assistance contributed to mitigating the psychological and social consequences of the operation. The successful collaboration between the Pakistani military and international partners serves as a valuable lesson for future counter-terrorism operations, emphasizing the importance of international collaboration and humanitarian efforts in achieving long-term stability and security.

Lessons Learned from International Collaboration in Counter-terrorism Operations

International collaboration plays a crucial role in counter-terrorism operations, as it allows countries to pool their resources, expertise, and intelligence to effectively combat militant groups. This subchapter will delve into the lessons learned from international collaboration in

Operation Zarb-e-Azb, the 2014-2017 Pakistani military operation against militant groups in North Waziristan.

One of the key lessons learned from international collaboration in counter-terrorism operations is the importance of information sharing. Operation Zarb-e-Azb saw Pakistan collaborating closely with the United States, Afghanistan, and other countries in sharing intelligence on militant groups. This exchange of information helped in identifying key targets, disrupting their networks, and preventing future attacks.

Another lesson learned is the significance of coordinated military operations. The success of Operation Zarb-e-Azb was largely attributed to the joint efforts of Pakistani military forces, intelligence agencies, and international partners. By synchronizing their actions and strategies, they were able to effectively target militant hideouts and dismantle their infrastructure.

Furthermore, international collaboration highlighted the need for a comprehensive approach to counter-terrorism. Operation Zarb-e-Azb not only involved military action but also focused on humanitarian challenges and relief efforts. International partners provided assistance and support in delivering aid and rebuilding infrastructure in the affected areas. This holistic approach helped in winning the trust and support of the local population, which is crucial in countering the influence of militant groups.

Additionally, international collaboration emphasized the significance of regional security dynamics. Operation Zarb-e-Azb had a profound impact on regional security, as it disrupted the safe havens of militant groups operating in North Waziristan. This operation served as a deterrent to other extremist organizations and sent a clear message that cooperation among nations is essential in combating terrorism.

Lastly, Operation Zarb-e-Azb highlighted the role of drone strikes in supporting counter-terrorism efforts. International collaboration allowed for the sharing of intelligence and coordination in conducting targeted drone strikes against high-value targets. These strikes proved to be effective in eliminating key leaders and disrupting the operational capabilities of militant groups.

In conclusion, international collaboration in counter-terrorism operations, as exemplified by Operation Zarb-e-Azb, has provided valuable lessons for future endeavors. The importance of information sharing, coordinated military operations, comprehensive approaches, regional security dynamics, and the use of drone strikes were all key takeaways from this collaborative effort. By applying these lessons, countries can enhance their capabilities and effectiveness in eliminating militant groups and ensuring global security.

Chapter 4: Humanitarian Challenges and Relief Efforts during Operation Zarb-e-Azb

Displacement of Civilians and Internally Displaced Persons (IDPs)

The military operation Zarb-e-Azb, conducted by the Pakistani military from 2014 to 2017 against militant groups in North Waziristan, had significant consequences for the civilian population. This subchapter focuses on the displacement of civilians and the challenges faced by Internally Displaced Persons (IDPs) during this operation.

Operation Zarb-e-Azb resulted in the mass displacement of civilians from North Waziristan. As the military engaged in intense combat with militant groups, the safety of the civilian population became a top priority. To ensure their protection, the authorities made the difficult decision to evacuate the affected areas. Tens of thousands of civilians were displaced from their homes, leaving behind their possessions and livelihoods.

The displacement of civilians created a humanitarian crisis, with IDPs facing numerous challenges. The sudden influx of displaced individuals overwhelmed the existing relief infrastructure, requiring immediate attention and support from local and international humanitarian organizations. The provision of basic necessities such as food, water, shelter, and healthcare became crucial in order to prevent a further humanitarian catastrophe.

Moreover, the psychological and social consequences of the displacement cannot be overlooked. Families were torn apart, children were separated from their parents, and communities were uprooted from their traditional way of life. The trauma experienced by IDPs cannot be underestimated, as they had to cope with the loss of their homes and the uncertainty of their future.

Despite these challenges, the Pakistani government, along with international partners, launched relief efforts to assist the IDPs. Temporary camps were set up to provide shelter and basic amenities. Aid agencies worked tirelessly to ensure that the affected population received the necessary support. The military played a crucial role in coordinating these relief efforts, working hand in hand with humanitarian organizations to ensure a smooth transition for the IDPs.

The displacement of civilians and the challenges faced by IDPs during Operation Zarb-e-Azb highlight the complex nature of military operations in counter-terrorism efforts. Balancing the need for security with the protection and welfare of civilians remains a formidable challenge. This chapter aims to shed light on the experiences of the displaced population and the lessons learned from this operation in order to inform future counter-terrorism operations and mitigate the impact on civilian communities.

Provision of Basic Necessities and Shelter to the Displaced

During Operation Zarb-e-Azb, the Pakistani military's battle against militant groups in North Waziristan, one of the key challenges faced was ensuring the provision of basic necessities and shelter to the displaced population. The large-scale military operation resulted in the displacement of thousands of families, leaving them in dire need of immediate assistance.

Recognizing the importance of addressing the humanitarian crisis, the Pakistani military, in collaboration with various national and international relief organizations, initiated a comprehensive relief effort to provide assistance to the affected communities. The primary focus was to ensure the provision of basic necessities such as food, clean water, healthcare, and shelter.

In the initial stages of the operation, the military established temporary displacement camps to accommodate the displaced families. These camps were equipped with basic amenities, including tents, bedding, and sanitation facilities, to provide a safe and secure environment for the affected population. Medical teams were also deployed to provide healthcare services and address any medical emergencies.

Furthermore, efforts were made to ensure the continuous supply of food and clean water to the displaced families. The military collaborated with humanitarian organizations to distribute ration packages and set up water filtration plants to meet the basic needs of the affected population. Schools and educational facilities were also established within the camps to ensure the continuation of education for children.

The provision of basic necessities and shelter to the displaced population was not without its challenges. The scale of displacement and the limited resources posed significant hurdles in delivering timely assistance. However, the Pakistani military, in coordination with relief organizations, worked tirelessly to overcome these challenges and ensure the well-being of the affected communities.

The provision of basic necessities and shelter to the displaced population during Operation Zarb-e-Azb not only addressed their immediate needs but also played a crucial role in winning the hearts and minds of the affected communities. By demonstrating their commitment to the welfare of the displaced, the military was able to build trust and support among the affected population, which in turn contributed to the overall success of the operation.

In conclusion, the provision of basic necessities and shelter to the displaced population was a critical aspect of Operation Zarb-e-Azb. The

Pakistani military, in collaboration with relief organizations, undertook significant efforts to ensure the well-being of the affected communities. By addressing the immediate humanitarian needs, the military not only alleviated the suffering of the displaced but also fostered a sense of trust and support among them, ultimately contributing to the success of the operation.

Healthcare and Medical Services in Conflict Areas

In the midst of conflict and turmoil, access to healthcare and medical services becomes a critical concern. This subchapter delves into the challenges faced in providing healthcare and medical assistance in conflict areas, specifically focusing on the context of Operation Zarb-e-Azb in North Waziristan. The chapter explores the efforts made by the Pakistani military and international collaborators to ensure the provision of essential medical services to the affected populations.

Operation Zarb-e-Azb, the Pakistani military's battle against militant groups in North Waziristan, not only aimed to eliminate terrorism but also sought to alleviate the suffering of the local communities. One of the key challenges faced during this operation was the dire state of healthcare infrastructure in the conflict-ridden region. Hospitals and clinics were either destroyed or severely damaged, making it extremely difficult to provide necessary medical assistance to the affected population.

Recognizing the urgency of the situation, the Pakistani military, in collaboration with international partners, launched a comprehensive healthcare and medical services plan. Mobile medical units were deployed to provide immediate medical aid to those in need. These units were equipped with essential medical supplies and staffed by qualified healthcare professionals who were dedicated to addressing the urgent healthcare needs of the affected population.

Additionally, efforts were made to rebuild and rehabilitate damaged healthcare facilities in the conflict areas. This included the reconstruction of hospitals and clinics, as well as the provision of medical equipment and supplies. The goal was not only to provide immediate medical assistance but also to ensure the sustainability of healthcare services in the long run.

Moreover, the subchapter examines the challenges faced by medical teams operating in conflict areas. The volatile security situation, limited resources, and the influx of displaced populations posed significant obstacles to providing healthcare services effectively. Despite these challenges, medical teams persevered, often putting their own lives at risk, to provide essential medical support to the affected population.

The subchapter concludes by highlighting the importance of international collaboration in addressing healthcare challenges in conflict areas. It emphasizes the need for sustained efforts to rebuild healthcare infrastructure, train local healthcare professionals, and ensure the availability of essential medical supplies. By addressing healthcare needs in conflict areas, Operation Zarb-e-Azb not only aimed to eliminate militant groups but also sought to provide relief and support to the affected communities.

In summary, this subchapter sheds light on the healthcare and medical services provided during Operation Zarb-e-Azb in North Waziristan. It explores the challenges faced, the efforts made by the Pakistani military and international collaborators, and the significance of healthcare in conflict areas. By understanding the complexities of providing healthcare in conflict zones, military historians can gain insights into the comprehensive approach undertaken during Operation Zarb-e-Azb and draw lessons for future counter-terrorism operations.

Education and Rehabilitation of Affected Children and Youth

One of the key aspects of any military operation, especially those aimed at countering militant groups, is the consideration of the long-term impact and consequences of the operation on the affected communities. Operation Zarb-e-Azb, the 2014-2017 Pakistani military operation against militant groups in North Waziristan, recognized the importance of addressing the needs of the affected children and youth.

The education and rehabilitation of affected children and youth became a crucial component of Operation Zarb-e-Azb's strategy. The operation aimed not only to eliminate the immediate threat posed by militant groups but also to pave the way for a brighter future for the younger generation. It was understood that without proper education and rehabilitation, these children and youth could become susceptible to extremist ideologies and recruitment by militant groups in the future.

The Pakistani military, in collaboration with local and international organizations, took significant steps to provide quality education and rehabilitation for the affected children and youth. Temporary schools were set up in safe areas to ensure uninterrupted education. Specialized teachers and counselors were deployed to address the psychological and social consequences experienced by these children and youth.

Efforts were made to offer vocational training programs, ensuring that the affected youth had access to skill development opportunities. By equipping them with practical skills, it was hoped that they would be able to reintegrate into society and lead productive lives.

Furthermore, Operation Zarb-e-Azb emphasized the importance of countering extremist ideologies through education. Curriculum reforms were undertaken to promote tolerance, peace, and critical thinking among the affected children and youth. This was seen as a long-term solution to preventing the recurrence of militancy in the region.

The education and rehabilitation of affected children and youth were not only seen as a humanitarian imperative but also as a strategic necessity. By investing in their future, Operation Zarb-e-Azb aimed to create a generation that would actively contribute to the stability and development of Pakistan, rather than being vulnerable to radicalization.

The success and effectiveness of Operation Zarb-e-Azb in eliminating militant groups cannot be fully evaluated without considering the long-term impact on the affected communities. Therefore, the focus on education and rehabilitation of affected children and youth serves as a testament to the comprehensive and holistic approach adopted by the Pakistani military in this operation. It provides valuable lessons for future counter-terrorism operations, emphasizing the importance of addressing the root causes of extremism and investing in the future of affected communities.

Role of Non-Governmental Organizations (NGOs) in Humanitarian Relief

In the context of Operation Zarb-e-Azb, the 2014-2017 Pakistani military operation against militant groups in North Waziristan, the role of non-governmental organizations (NGOs) in humanitarian relief cannot be underestimated. These organizations have played a crucial role in providing assistance, support, and relief to the affected communities during and after the operation. Military historians, as well as those interested in the impact of Operation Zarb-e-Azb on counter-terrorism efforts in Pakistan, need to understand and appreciate the contributions of NGOs in order to gain a comprehensive understanding of the operation's dynamics and outcomes.

NGOs have been at the forefront of delivering humanitarian aid to the affected communities in North Waziristan. They have provided essential services such as healthcare, food, clean water, shelter, and education to the displaced population. NGOs have also played a significant role in coordinating relief efforts with government agencies, international organizations, and local communities, ensuring that aid reaches those in need effectively and efficiently.

One of the key strengths of NGOs is their ability to operate independently and impartially, ensuring that humanitarian assistance reaches all affected communities, regardless of their background or affiliation. This has been particularly important in Operation Zarb-e-Azb, where the conflict has caused displacement and suffering among diverse communities.

NGOs have also played a vital role in addressing the psychological and social consequences of the operation on affected communities. They have provided psychosocial support and counseling services to help individuals and communities cope with trauma and rebuild their lives. By addressing the social and psychological needs of the affected communities, NGOs have contributed to the long-term healing and recovery process.

Furthermore, NGOs have been instrumental in advocating for the rights and protection of the affected populations. They have raised awareness about the human rights violations and abuses that may have occurred during the operation, ensuring that the voices and concerns of the affected communities are heard and addressed.

In conclusion, the role of NGOs in humanitarian relief during Operation Zarb-e-Azb has been indispensable. Their ability to provide essential services, coordinate relief efforts, address psychological and social consequences, and advocate for the rights of the affected populations has contributed significantly to the overall success and effectiveness of the operation. Military historians and those interested in understanding the impact of counter-terrorism efforts in Pakistan must acknowledge and study the role of NGOs in order to gain a comprehensive understanding of the operation's complexities and outcomes.

Chapter 5: Psychological and Social Consequences of Operation Zarb-e-Azb on Affected Communities

Trauma and Post-Traumatic Stress Disorder (PTSD) Among Civilians

The 2014-2017 Pakistani military operation, Zarb-e-Azb, against militant groups in North Waziristan had far-reaching consequences not only on the security dynamics of the region but also on the lives of the civilians residing in the conflict-ridden area. This subchapter aims to shed light on the trauma and post-traumatic stress disorder (PTSD) experienced by civilians as a result of this operation.

During Operation Zarb-e-Azb, the Pakistani military launched a comprehensive offensive against militant groups, aiming to eliminate their presence from North Waziristan. However, the intensity of the conflict and the displacement of thousands of civilians had a profound impact on the mental health of the affected communities. The indiscriminate use of force, constant fear, and witnessing violent acts took a toll on the psychological well-being of the local population.

Trauma and PTSD became prevalent among civilians who experienced or witnessed traumatic events during the operation. The symptoms of PTSD, such as flashbacks, nightmares, anxiety, and social withdrawal, were common among the affected individuals. The trauma caused by Operation Zarb-e-Azb not only affected adults but also had a lasting impact on children, who experienced disrupted education, loss of loved ones, and a sense of insecurity.

The mental health consequences of the operation were exacerbated by the lack of adequate mental health services and support systems in the region. The affected communities faced significant challenges in accessing psychological care and support, further worsening their condition. This subchapter will explore the role of humanitarian organizations and relief efforts in addressing the psychological and social consequences of Operation Zarb-e-Azb and providing support to the affected population.

Furthermore, it will discuss the importance of recognizing and addressing trauma and PTSD in post-conflict situations to ensure the well-being and recovery of the affected communities. The chapter will also highlight the need for long-term rehabilitation programs, including therapy and counseling, to tackle the psychological consequences of conflict.

In conclusion, the trauma and PTSD experienced by civilians during Operation Zarb-e-Azb had a significant impact on their lives. It is crucial for military historians and those interested in the impact of counter-terrorism operations to understand the psychological and social consequences of such conflicts on affected communities. By recognizing and addressing the trauma experienced by civilians, future counter-terrorism operations can be conducted with greater consideration for the mental health and well-being of the affected population.

Disruption of Social Fabric and Community Structures

The military operation Zarb-e-Azb, conducted by the Pakistani military between 2014 and 2017, had a significant impact on the social fabric and community structures in North Waziristan. This subchapter aims to explore the consequences of the operation, shedding light on the disruptions and challenges faced by the affected communities.

One of the key effects of Zarb-e-Azb was the displacement of a large number of people from their homes. The operation resulted in the mass exodus of civilians, who had to leave behind their belongings and livelihoods in search of safety. This displacement not only disrupted the social fabric of these communities but also created a burden on neighboring areas, straining already limited resources.

Moreover, the military operation led to the destruction of infrastructure, including homes, schools, and healthcare facilities. This had a profound impact on the affected communities, further exacerbating their vulnerabilities. Disrupted education and healthcare systems, along with the loss of employment opportunities, created an environment of uncertainty and despair among the local population.

Furthermore, the operation also caused a breakdown in traditional community structures. The displacement and destruction of homes forced families and communities to separate, scattering them across different regions. This separation disrupted the sense of community and belonging, which are crucial for the social fabric of any society. Additionally, the operation also targeted militant safe havens, which were often embedded within local communities. The removal of these elements further disrupted the dynamics within these communities.

The disruption of social fabric and community structures had lasting psychological and social consequences on the affected population. Many individuals experienced trauma, loss, and displacement, leading to increased rates of mental health issues, including anxiety and depression. The breakdown of community structures also contributed to a sense of isolation and alienation among the affected population, hindering their ability to recover and rebuild their lives.

In conclusion, the military operation Zarb-e-Azb had significant repercussions on the social fabric and community structures in North Waziristan. The displacement of people, destruction of infrastructure, and breakdown of traditional community structures disrupted the lives of the affected population. Addressing the social and psychological consequences of the operation is crucial to ensure the long-term stability and well-being of these communities.

Stigmatization and Discrimination Faced by Displaced Persons

One of the lesser-known aspects of Operation Zarb-e-Azb, the 2014-2017 Pakistani military operation against militant groups in North Waziristan, is the stigmatization and discrimination faced by the displaced persons. As military historians, it is crucial to shed light on this issue and understand its implications for future counter-terrorism operations.

During Operation Zarb-e-Azb, thousands of individuals were displaced from their homes and forced to seek refuge in other parts of Pakistan. These displaced persons, primarily belonging to the local communities, faced numerous challenges, including stigmatization and discrimination.

The stigma attached to being a displaced person often arises from misconceptions and stereotypes perpetuated by society. Displaced individuals are often viewed as potential terrorists or sympathizers of militant groups due to their geographical proximity to conflict zones. This stigma not only affects their social standing but also impacts their access to basic services such as healthcare, education, and employment opportunities.

Additionally, discrimination against displaced persons exacerbates their already precarious situation. They may face difficulties in finding adequate housing, encountering biases in the job market, and being subjected to harassment or violence. Discrimination against these individuals can lead to a sense of exclusion, further alienating them from the society they once called home.

Furthermore, the psychological and social consequences of stigmatization and discrimination on affected communities cannot be underestimated. Displaced persons may experience a loss of identity, feelings of shame, and a sense of hopelessness. These negative emotions can hinder their ability to rebuild their lives and contribute to the social fabric of their new communities.

To address this issue, it is essential for military and humanitarian actors to work together to combat stigmatization and discrimination faced by displaced persons. This can be achieved through awareness campaigns that challenge stereotypes and promote inclusivity. Providing equal access to basic services and opportunities for displaced individuals is also crucial in fostering their social integration.

By acknowledging and addressing the stigmatization and discrimination faced by displaced persons during Operation Zarb-e-Azb, we can learn valuable lessons for future counter-terrorism operations. It is imperative to prioritize the protection and well-being of affected communities not only during military operations but also in the post-conflict phase. Only by doing so can we ensure a more just and inclusive society for all.

Efforts Towards Psycho-Social Support and Rehabilitation

The military operation Zarb-e-Azb, conducted by the Pakistani military against militant groups in North Waziristan from 2014 to 2017, not only aimed at eliminating the threat of terrorism but also recognized the importance of addressing the psychological and social consequences faced by affected communities. This subchapter delves into the efforts made towards psycho-social support and rehabilitation during and after Operation Zarb-e-Azb.

Recognizing the immense impact of conflict on individuals and communities, the Pakistani military took proactive measures to provide psycho-social support to the affected populations. A range of initiatives were undertaken to address the psychological trauma experienced by both civilians and military personnel. Specialized teams of psychologists and social workers were deployed to provide counseling and therapy to individuals suffering from post-traumatic stress disorder (PTSD) and other mental health issues.

In addition to the immediate psychological support, rehabilitation programs were implemented to help individuals reintegrate into society. These programs focused on skill development, vocational training, and providing economic opportunities to the affected populations. By equipping individuals with the necessary skills and support, the aim was to enable them to rebuild their lives and contribute positively to society.

Furthermore, efforts were made to rebuild social structures and strengthen community bonds that had been severely disrupted by the conflict. Community-based initiatives were launched to promote cohesion, resilience, and social harmony. These initiatives included the establishment of community centers, sports facilities, and cultural events to foster a sense of normalcy and belonging.

The success of these psycho-social support and rehabilitation efforts can be attributed to the collaboration between various stakeholders. International organizations, NGOs, and civil society groups played a critical role in providing expertise, resources, and funding to ensure the implementation and sustainability of these programs.

Despite the challenges faced during and after Operation Zarb-e-Azb, the concerted efforts towards psycho-social support and rehabilitation have helped in mitigating the long-term consequences of the conflict. By addressing the psychological and social needs of affected communities, the Pakistani military has not only focused on eliminating militant groups but also on healing and rebuilding the lives of those impacted by the conflict.

This subchapter highlights the significance of integrating psycho-social support and rehabilitation efforts into future counter-terrorism operations. It emphasizes the need for a holistic approach that recognizes the importance of addressing the psychological and social consequences of conflict, ultimately contributing to the long-term stability and well-being of affected populations.

Chapter 6: Evaluating the Success and Effectiveness of Operation Zarb-e-Azb in Eliminating Militant Groups

Assessment of Militant Group Presence and Activities Pre-Operation Zarb-e-Azb

In order to understand the significance and impact of Operation Zarb-e-Azb, it is crucial to assess the presence and activities of militant groups in North Waziristan before the military operation took place. This assessment provides important context and sheds light on the challenges faced by the Pakistani military and intelligence agencies in combating these groups.

Prior to Operation Zarb-e-Azb, North Waziristan had become a safe haven for various militant groups, including Tehrik-i-Taliban Pakistan (TTP), Haqqani Network, and foreign fighters affiliated with Al-Qaeda. The region served as a breeding ground for extremist ideologies and a base for launching attacks on Pakistani soil and beyond. These groups had established a complex network of training camps, command and control centers, and hideouts, making it difficult for the security forces to target them effectively.

Militant activities in North Waziristan were not limited to planning and executing terrorist attacks. They also had a significant influence on the local population, exerting control over the region through a combination of coercion and propaganda. The presence of these groups had resulted in the displacement of thousands of people, as they lived under constant fear and oppression.

Furthermore, the militants had forged alliances with other extremist organizations, both within Pakistan and across the border in Afghanistan. This cross-border collaboration facilitated the movement of fighters, weapons, and resources, posing a serious threat to regional security.

The assessment of militant group presence and activities pre-Operation Zarb-e-Azb highlights the immense challenge faced by the Pakistani military. It underscores the need for a comprehensive and decisive military operation to dismantle the infrastructure and capabilities of these groups.

Operation Zarb-e-Azb, launched in June 2014, aimed to eliminate these militant groups and restore peace and stability in North Waziristan. The operation utilized a combination of ground offensives, airstrikes, and intelligence-driven operations to target militant hideouts and disrupt their command and control structure.

Assessing the pre-operation scenario provides a benchmark for evaluating the success and effectiveness of Operation Zarb-e-Azb in eliminating militant groups. It also helps in understanding the lessons learned from this operation for future counter-terrorism efforts.

In conclusion, the assessment of militant group presence and activities pre-Operation Zarb-e-Azb provides a critical understanding of the security landscape in North Waziristan. It highlights the grave threat posed by these groups and the need for a comprehensive military operation to restore peace and stability in the region.

Analysis of Militant Group Elimination and Neutralization During Operation Zarb-e-Azb

Operation Zarb-e-Azb stands out as a significant milestone in the Pakistani military's battle against militant groups in North Waziristan. This subchapter aims to provide a comprehensive analysis of the strategies and tactics employed during the operation to eliminate and neutralize these militant groups.

One of the key factors contributing to the success of Operation Zarb-e-Azb was the meticulous planning and execution carried out by the Pakistani military and its intelligence agencies. Extensive intelligence gathering and analysis helped identify the locations and strongholds of various militant groups, enabling precise targeting and minimizing collateral damage. This approach proved vital in dismantling the infrastructure and command structures of these groups.

Furthermore, the operation showcased the effectiveness of international collaboration in combating terrorism. Support from the United States and other regional allies in terms of intelligence sharing and logistical assistance greatly enhanced the operation's impact. The coordinated efforts of these international partners facilitated the rapid neutralization of high-value targets and disrupted the supply lines of militant groups.

While Operation Zarb-e-Azb primarily focused on eliminating militant groups, it also recognized the importance of humanitarian challenges and relief efforts. The Pakistani military, in collaboration with national and international humanitarian organizations, worked diligently to provide assistance and support to the affected communities. The provision of medical aid, food, and shelter helped alleviate the suffering of the displaced population.

However, it is crucial to acknowledge the psychological and social consequences faced by the affected communities. The operation's intensity and scale inevitably led to displacement, trauma, and disruption of normalcy. Addressing these challenges and providing psychosocial support to affected individuals and communities became an integral part of the operation's overall strategy.

Evaluating the success and effectiveness of Operation Zarb-e-Azb requires a comprehensive analysis of the outcomes achieved. While the operation significantly weakened the militant groups in North Waziristan and disrupted their ability to launch large-scale attacks, it is essential to acknowledge that some elements may have relocated to other regions. Continued vigilance and sustained counter-terrorism efforts are necessary to prevent their resurgence.

In conclusion, Operation Zarb-e-Azb serves as a valuable case study for military historians and individuals interested in the dynamics of counter-terrorism operations. Its success can be attributed to meticulous planning, international collaboration, humanitarian efforts, and the recognition of psychological and social consequences. Analyzing the strategies and lessons learned from this operation will undoubtedly contribute to the development of more effective approaches in future counter-terrorism endeavors.

Evaluation of Counter-terrorism Strategies and Tactics Employed

The subchapter titled "Evaluation of Counter-terrorism Strategies and Tactics Employed" delves into an in-depth analysis of the operational and tactical approaches adopted by the Pakistani military during Operation Zarb-e-Azb. This evaluation is of utmost importance to military historians and experts in the field, as it provides critical insights into the effectiveness of these strategies and tactics in combating militant groups in North Waziristan.

Operation Zarb-e-Azb, conducted by the Pakistani military from 2014 to 2017, aimed to eliminate the presence of militant groups in the region and restore peace and stability. The counter-terrorism strategies employed during this operation were multifaceted, combining intelligence-driven operations, precision airstrikes, ground offensives, and close coordination with international partners.

This subchapter begins by examining the intelligence agencies' role in planning and executing Operation Zarb-e-Azb. It highlights the significance of accurate and timely intelligence in successfully targeting militant hideouts and disrupting their networks. The evaluation also explores the collaboration between Pakistani intelligence agencies and their international counterparts, emphasizing the importance of such partnerships in gathering intelligence and sharing resources.

Furthermore, the subchapter evaluates the effectiveness of the strategies employed, including the utilization of drone strikes to support ground operations. It discusses the advantages and limitations of drone strikes in targeting high-value individuals and disrupting militant activities.

Additionally, the evaluation assesses the success of Operation Zarb-e-Azb in eliminating militant groups and its impact on regional security dynamics. It analyzes the broader implications of this military operation on neighboring countries and the overall security situation in the region.

The subchapter also delves into the humanitarian challenges and relief efforts during Operation Zarb-e-Azb, acknowledging the importance of addressing the needs of affected communities. It explores the psychological and social consequences of the operation on these communities, shedding light on the long-term impact and the measures taken to mitigate these effects.

Finally, the subchapter concludes by drawing lessons from Operation Zarb-e-Azb for future counter-terrorism operations. It highlights the strengths and weaknesses of the employed strategies and tactics, providing valuable insights for military planners and policymakers.

Overall, this subchapter serves as a comprehensive evaluation of the counter-terrorism strategies and tactics employed during Operation Zarb-e-Azb. It offers a nuanced understanding of the operational effectiveness, challenges faced, and lessons learned from this significant military operation, making it a vital resource for military historians and experts in the field.

Comparison of Operation Zarb-e-Azb with Previous Counter-terrorism Operations in Pakistan

In the subchapter titled "Comparison of Operation Zarb-e-Azb with Previous Counter-terrorism Operations in Pakistan," this section aims to provide military historians with an insightful analysis of how Operation Zarb-e-Azb differed from past counter-terrorism operations in Pakistan. By examining the similarities and differences, this subchapter sheds light on the unique aspects of Zarb-e-Azb that contributed to its success and effectiveness in combating militant groups in North Waziristan.

One significant distinction of Operation Zarb-e-Azb was its comprehensive and coordinated approach. Unlike previous operations that focused primarily on military force, Zarb-e-Azb incorporated multiple elements such as intelligence gathering, strategic planning, and international collaboration. This holistic approach enabled the Pakistani military to disrupt the operational capabilities of militant groups more effectively.

Furthermore, the extensive use of precision airstrikes and drone strikes played a crucial role in Zarb-e-Azb's success. These technologies not only minimized collateral damage but also targeted key militant leaders and infrastructure, significantly weakening their operational capabilities. By leveraging these advanced tactics, Zarb-e-Azb achieved a higher level of precision and efficiency compared to previous operations.

Additionally, Operation Zarb-e-Azb prioritized the protection and welfare of affected communities. The military made concerted efforts to minimize civilian casualties and provided humanitarian aid and relief to the displaced population. This approach not only demonstrated the military's commitment to safeguarding innocent lives but also helped win the hearts and minds of the local population, undermining the support for militant groups.

Furthermore, Zarb-e-Azb benefited from improved intelligence sharing and cooperation with international partners. The collaboration with intelligence agencies from various countries, particularly the United States, facilitated the identification and targeting of high-value militant targets. This international collaboration enhanced the effectiveness and reach of Zarb-e-Azb, making it a more formidable force against militant groups.

In conclusion, Operation Zarb-e-Azb set itself apart from previous counter-terrorism operations in Pakistan through its comprehensive approach, the use of advanced technologies, a focus on protecting affected communities, and enhanced international collaboration. By analyzing these differences, military historians can gain valuable insights into the successful strategies employed in Zarb-e-Azb and extract lessons that can be applied to future counter-terrorism operations.

Chapter 7: The Role of Intelligence Agencies in Planning and Executing Operation Zarb-e-Azb

Intelligence Gathering and Analysis Prior to Operation Zarb-e-Azb

In the subchapter "Intelligence Gathering and Analysis Prior to Operation Zarb-e-Azb," we delve into the crucial role that intelligence played in the planning and execution of the Pakistani military's battle against militant groups in North Waziristan. This chapter aims to provide military historians with an in-depth understanding of the intelligence operations that paved the way for Operation Zarb-e-Azb.

Before the initiation of Operation Zarb-e-Azb, extensive intelligence gathering and analysis were conducted by Pakistani intelligence agencies. The primary objective was to identify the locations, strength, and capabilities of the militant groups operating in North Waziristan. This phase involved a coordinated effort between various intelligence agencies, including Inter-Services Intelligence (ISI), Military Intelligence (MI), and the Intelligence Bureau (IB).

Intelligence agents infiltrated the region, establishing human intelligence networks to gather accurate and actionable information. They focused on developing sources within the local population, leveraging their knowledge of the area, and building relationships of trust. Satellite imagery, signal intelligence, and electronic surveillance were also utilized to gather critical data.

The gathered intelligence was then analyzed by a team of experts who assessed the credibility and reliability of the information. This analysis played a vital role in identifying high-value targets, locating militant hideouts, and determining the appropriate military strategy to neutralize the threat effectively.

The intelligence gathered also provided valuable insights into the logistical infrastructure of the militant groups, including their communication networks, supply lines, and weapons caches. This information was crucial in planning precise and targeted operations, minimizing collateral damage while maximizing the impact on the militant groups.

Furthermore, intelligence analysis helped in understanding the complex dynamics between different militant groups and their affiliations with external entities. This knowledge enabled the military to anticipate the potential reactions and responses of the militants during the operation.

The success of Operation Zarb-e-Azb can largely be attributed to the comprehensive intelligence gathering and analysis that preceded it. The meticulous planning based on accurate intelligence allowed the Pakistani military to swiftly execute targeted operations, leading to significant victories against militant groups in North Waziristan.

In conclusion, the subchapter "Intelligence Gathering and Analysis Prior to Operation Zarb-e-Azb" sheds light on the vital role played by intelligence agencies in the planning and execution of this major military operation. The intelligence gathered, and subsequent analysis provided the foundation for successful military strategies, enabling the Pakistani military to effectively eliminate militant groups in North Waziristan. This chapter serves as an essential resource for military historians interested in understanding the intricate details of Operation Zarb-e-Azb and its impact on counter-terrorism efforts in Pakistan.

Covert Operations and Targeted Killings of High-Value Targets

In the relentless pursuit of dismantling and eliminating militant groups in North Waziristan, Operation Zarb-e-Azb employed a range of strategies, including covert operations and targeted killings of high-value targets. This subchapter delves into the intricacies and significance of these operations, offering military historians a comprehensive understanding of the tactics employed during this pivotal period in Pakistan's counter-terrorism efforts.

Covert operations, characterized by their secrecy and discretion, played a crucial role in Operation Zarb-e-Azb. These operations were conducted by highly trained special forces, who infiltrated militant networks, gathering intelligence, and identifying high-value targets. Such operations allowed the Pakistani military to strike swiftly and efficiently, neutralizing key figures within militant organizations, disrupting their command structures, and severely hampering their ability to carry out attacks.

The targeted killings of high-value targets were a vital component of Operation Zarb-e-Azb. These individuals, often leaders or key operatives within militant groups, possessed considerable influence and operational capabilities. By eliminating them, the Pakistani military dealt a severe blow to the militants' ability to regroup and launch further attacks. Moreover, the removal of high-value targets undermined the morale and cohesion of these groups, leading to internal divisions and a decline in their overall effectiveness.

The success of covert operations and targeted killings was dependent on a robust intelligence apparatus. Intelligence agencies, both domestic and international, played a critical role in planning and executing these operations. Their expertise in gathering, analyzing, and disseminating intelligence was vital in identifying high-value targets, understanding their networks, and exploiting their vulnerabilities. Furthermore, international collaboration in intelligence sharing and joint operations bolstered the effectiveness and impact of these covert operations.

However, it is essential to acknowledge the ethical and legal implications of covert operations and targeted killings. While these tactics were instrumental in dismantling militant groups, they also raised questions surrounding human rights, due process, and accountability. The subchapter explores these complexities, providing an objective analysis of the challenges and potential drawbacks associated with such operations.

Covert operations and targeted killings of high-value targets formed a critical pillar of Operation Zarb-e-Azb. By shedding light on the strategies employed, this subchapter offers military historians a comprehensive understanding of the operational dynamics and the impact of these tactics on the overall success of the Pakistani military's battle against militant groups in North Waziristan.

Collaboration between Intelligence Agencies and Armed Forces

The collaboration between intelligence agencies and armed forces played a crucial role in the success of Operation Zarb-e-Azb, the 2014-2017 Pakistani military operation against militant groups in North Waziristan. This subchapter focuses on the significance of this collaboration and its impact on the overall operation, particularly in terms of intelligence gathering, planning, and execution.

Intelligence agencies, such as the Inter-Services Intelligence (ISI) and Military Intelligence (MI), worked closely with the armed forces to gather critical information on the locations, activities, and capabilities of militant groups in North Waziristan. Through their extensive networks and intelligence-sharing arrangements with international partners, these agencies provided valuable insights into the complex dynamics of militant networks operating in the region.

The intelligence gathered by these agencies formed the foundation for the planning and execution of military operations. Armed forces utilized this information to identify high-value targets, plan targeted strikes, and coordinate ground operations effectively. The collaboration between intelligence agencies and armed forces ensured that the military had accurate and up-to-date information, enabling them to take precise action against militant groups.

Moreover, intelligence agencies also played a vital role in the coordination of international collaborations. They facilitated cooperation and information sharing with international partners, such as the United States and Afghanistan, who supported Operation Zarb-e-Azb. This collaboration enhanced the effectiveness of the operation by providing access to advanced technology, intelligence resources, and expertise.

The synergy between intelligence agencies and armed forces was essential not only during the execution of Operation Zarb-e-Azb but also in the post-operation phase. Intelligence agencies continued to monitor the activities of militant groups, both locally and internationally, to prevent their resurgence and plan future counter-terrorism operations.

In conclusion, the collaboration between intelligence agencies and armed forces was a critical factor in the success of Operation Zarb-e-Azb. Their joint efforts in intelligence gathering, planning, and execution ensured precise and effective action against militant groups in North Waziristan. This subchapter provides insights into the significance of this collaboration and highlights its impact on the overall success of the operation. Military historians and those interested in the niches of Operation Zarb-e-Azb and counter-terrorism efforts will find this subchapter invaluable in understanding the importance of intelligence agencies in modern military operations and the lessons learned for future counter-terrorism endeavors.

Lessons Learned in Intelligence Coordination and Sharing

Intelligence coordination and sharing played a pivotal role in the success of Operation Zarb-e-Azb, the Pakistani military's battle against militant groups in North Waziristan from 2014 to 2017. This subchapter delves into the valuable lessons learned in this aspect, highlighting the importance of effective intelligence gathering, collaboration, and information sharing for future counter-terrorism operations.

One of the key lessons learned was the need for enhanced cooperation between different intelligence agencies. Operation Zarb-e-Azb brought together multiple intelligence agencies, including the Inter-Services Intelligence (ISI), Military Intelligence (MI), and Intelligence Bureau (IB), among others. The collaboration between these agencies allowed for a comprehensive understanding of the militant groups' operations, capabilities, and networks. This coordination also facilitated the exchange of critical information, enabling the military to plan and execute precise and targeted operations.

Another important lesson was the significance of international collaboration. Operation Zarb-e-Azb benefited from intelligence sharing and support from international partners, particularly the United States and Afghanistan. The sharing of actionable intelligence and joint operations proved instrumental in tracking down and eliminating high-value targets. This cooperation not only enhanced the effectiveness of the operation but also forged stronger relations between Pakistan and its international partners in the fight against terrorism.

Furthermore, the subchapter explores the importance of incorporating technological advancements in intelligence gathering and sharing. Operation Zarb-e-Azb witnessed the use of modern surveillance equipment, unmanned aerial vehicles (UAVs), and communication systems. These technologies provided real-time information, enabling the military to respond swiftly and effectively to changing dynamics on the ground.

Additionally, the subchapter highlights the need for continuous evaluation and improvement of intelligence coordination and sharing mechanisms. Regular communication, joint exercises, and training programs among intelligence agencies can enhance their capabilities and ensure seamless coordination during future operations.

Ultimately, the lessons learned in intelligence coordination and sharing during Operation Zarb-e-Azb serve as a valuable guide for military historians and policymakers. By analyzing these experiences, future counter-terrorism efforts can be strengthened, ensuring that intelligence agencies work together seamlessly and share critical information to effectively combat militant groups. This subchapter sheds light on the significance of intelligence coordination and sharing, emphasizing its role in achieving success in counter-terrorism operations.

Chapter 8: Operation Zarb-e-Azb and its Impact on Regional Security Dynamics

Disruption of Cross-Border Militant Activities and Safe Havens

One of the key objectives of Operation Zarb-e-Azb was to disrupt cross-border militant activities and eliminate safe havens for militant groups in North Waziristan. This subchapter delves into the strategies and tactics employed by the Pakistani military to achieve this goal, as well as the challenges they faced in their mission.

The border region between Pakistan and Afghanistan has long been a hotbed for militant activities, with various extremist groups using it as a safe haven to plan and launch attacks. Operation Zarb-e-Azb aimed to dismantle this infrastructure and sever the connections between these groups and their supporters.

To disrupt cross-border militant activities, the Pakistani military employed a multi-pronged approach. They conducted targeted airstrikes on militant hideouts and training camps, effectively destroying their infrastructure. Ground forces then moved in to clear the area and apprehend or eliminate the remaining militants.

The operation also focused on securing the border, with increased deployment of troops and the construction of border forts. This was crucial in preventing militants from freely crossing the border and regrouping in Afghanistan.

International collaboration played a significant role in disrupting cross-border militant activities. The Pakistani military worked closely with their Afghan counterparts, sharing intelligence and coordinating operations. The United States also provided support through drone strikes, targeting high-value militants and disrupting their leadership structures.

However, the operation was not without challenges. The rugged and mountainous terrain of North Waziristan posed logistical difficulties for the military. Moreover, the porous border allowed militants to escape into Afghanistan, leading to concerns of a potential resurgence in the future.

Despite these challenges, Operation Zarb-e-Azb achieved significant success in disrupting cross-border militant activities and eliminating safe havens. It dealt a major blow to militant groups, severely limiting their ability to operate and launch attacks. The operation also sent a strong message to the international community about Pakistan's commitment to countering terrorism.

The disruption of cross-border militant activities and safe havens has had a profound impact on regional security dynamics. It has not only made the border region more secure but has also contributed to the overall stability of Pakistan and Afghanistan. The success of Operation Zarb-e-Azb serves as a valuable lesson for future counter-terrorism operations, emphasizing the importance of international collaboration, intelligence sharing, and a comprehensive approach to tackling militant groups.

Implications for Afghan-Pakistan Relations and Border Security

The military operation Zarb-e-Azb, conducted by the Pakistani military against militant groups in North Waziristan from 2014 to 2017, had far-reaching implications for Afghan-Pakistan relations and border security. This subchapter explores the various dimensions of these implications, shedding light on the complex dynamics between the two neighboring countries and their efforts to address the common challenge of terrorism.

One of the key implications of Operation Zarb-e-Azb on Afghan-Pakistan relations was the increased cooperation and coordination between the two countries' militaries. The operation served as a wake-up call for both sides, highlighting the need for joint efforts in combating terrorism. The intelligence sharing and joint operations that ensued not only improved border security but also fostered a sense of trust and understanding between the two nations.

However, the operation also faced challenges in terms of border security. The porous border between Afghanistan and Pakistan has long been a haven for militants, allowing them to freely cross and launch attacks on both sides. Operation Zarb-e-Azb aimed to address this security vacuum by establishing a more robust border control mechanism. While significant progress was made, the task of completely securing the border remains a daunting challenge due to its rugged terrain and the presence of various militant groups.

Furthermore, the implications of Operation Zarb-e-Azb on Afghan-Pakistan relations extended beyond the military realm. The operation had a profound impact on the Afghan refugees residing in Pakistan. As a result of the operation, a large number of Afghan refugees were displaced, adding to the existing humanitarian challenges in the region. This influx of refugees strained the already fragile Afghan-Pakistan relations and further complicated the efforts to address the root causes of terrorism.

In conclusion, Operation Zarb-e-Azb had significant implications for Afghan-Pakistan relations and border security. While it led to increased cooperation and coordination between the two nations' militaries, challenges in border security and the displacement of Afghan refugees posed significant hurdles. Understanding these implications is crucial for military historians to assess the overall effectiveness of the operation and draw valuable lessons for future counter-terrorism operations in the region.

Regional Repercussions and Cooperation in Counter-terrorism Efforts

The success of any counter-terrorism operation depends not only on the efforts of one country, but also on regional cooperation and the collective action of multiple nations. This subchapter explores the regional repercussions and cooperation that took place during Operation Zarb-e-Azb, the Pakistani military's battle against militant groups in North Waziristan from 2014 to 2017.

Operation Zarb-e-Azb had significant implications for regional security dynamics. The operation disrupted the safe havens and networks of militant groups not only in Pakistan but also in neighboring countries. The porous borders between Pakistan and Afghanistan allowed militant groups to freely cross and operate, thus cooperation between the two countries was crucial. The operation highlighted the need for intelligence sharing, joint operations, and coordination between Pakistan and Afghanistan to effectively combat terrorism.

Furthermore, Operation Zarb-e-Azb also brought together other regional players, such as the United States, China, and Iran, who recognized the importance of eliminating terrorist threats in the region. These countries provided various forms of assistance, including intelligence sharing, military aid, and training, which significantly bolstered the operation. The collaboration between Pakistan and these regional players not only strengthened counter-terrorism efforts but also had a positive impact on regional security.

The subchapter delves into the challenges and achievements of regional cooperation during Operation Zarb-e-Azb. It examines how the operation led to increased collaboration between Pakistan and Afghanistan, as well as the role of international partners in supporting the operation. The analysis also highlights the lessons learned from this regional cooperation and its implications for future counter-terrorism operations.

Additionally, the subchapter explores the impact of Operation Zarb-e-Azb on regional security dynamics. It discusses how the operation disrupted the flow of militants and weapons across borders, thereby reducing the threat to regional stability. The role of intelligence agencies in planning and executing the operation is also examined, shedding light on the importance of intelligence sharing and cooperation in counter-terrorism efforts.

Overall, this subchapter provides a comprehensive analysis of the regional repercussions and cooperation witnessed during Operation Zarb-e-Azb. It emphasizes the importance of collective action and collaboration in effectively combating terrorism and maintaining regional security. By examining the lessons learned from this operation, military historians and experts can gain valuable insights into the dynamics of counter-terrorism efforts and apply them to future operations.

Challenges and Future Prospects for Regional Security Cooperation

In the subchapter "Challenges and Future Prospects for Regional Security Cooperation," we delve into the complexities and opportunities for collaboration among regional stakeholders in the context of Operation Zarb-e-Azb. This section aims to provide military historians with a comprehensive understanding of the challenges faced during the operation and the potential for future security cooperation in the region.

Operation Zarb-e-Azb, the 2014-2017 Pakistani military operation against militant groups in North Waziristan, was a landmark event in Pakistan's fight against terrorism. While the operation achieved significant success in eliminating militant groups in the region, the challenges encountered during the operation highlighted the need for enhanced regional security cooperation.

One of the key challenges was the porous border between Pakistan and Afghanistan, which allowed militants to freely cross and launch attacks on both sides. This necessitated greater collaboration between the Pakistani and Afghan security forces to effectively secure the border and prevent cross-border terrorism. Furthermore, the operation also exposed the existence of safe havens for militants in neighboring countries, emphasizing the importance of regional cooperation in dismantling such networks.

Another challenge was the role of external actors in supporting militant groups. The operation exposed the complexities of regional dynamics and the need for coordinated efforts to address the root causes of terrorism. This highlights the importance of international collaboration to counter the financing, training, and arming of militant groups operating in the region.

Despite these challenges, Operation Zarb-e-Azb also presents an opportunity for future regional security cooperation. The success of the operation demonstrated the effectiveness of a joint military strategy against militant groups. This could serve as a model for future counter-terrorism operations in the region, with participating countries pooling their resources and intelligence to achieve common objectives.

Furthermore, Operation Zarb-e-Azb highlighted the significance of humanitarian challenges and relief efforts in conflict-affected areas. Cooperation in these areas can not only provide much-needed assistance to affected communities but also foster trust and goodwill among regional stakeholders.

In conclusion, the challenges faced during Operation Zarb-e-Azb underscore the need for enhanced regional security cooperation. By addressing the porous borders, countering external support for militant groups, and focusing on humanitarian relief efforts, regional stakeholders can create a more secure and stable environment. Operation Zarb-e-Azb serves as a valuable lesson for future counter-terrorism operations, offering insights into the importance of intelligence sharing, joint military strategies, and collaborative efforts in ensuring regional security.

Chapter 9: Media Coverage and Public Perception of Operation Zarb-e-Azb in Pakistan

Media Access and Reporting Restrictions during Operation Zarb-e-Azb

During Operation Zarb-e-Azb, the Pakistani military's battle against militant groups in North Waziristan, media access and reporting restrictions played a significant role in shaping public perception and understanding of the operation. This subchapter aims to shed light on the challenges faced by media professionals and the impact it had on the dissemination of information during this critical military operation.

Understandably, the Pakistani government imposed strict reporting restrictions to maintain operational security and prevent the leakage of sensitive information to the enemy. This meant that journalists and media organizations faced numerous hurdles in accessing the conflict zone and reporting on the ground realities. The military's control over information flow limited the ability of media personnel to independently verify facts and present a comprehensive picture of the operation.

However, it is important to note that the military did make efforts to facilitate media coverage within the limitations imposed by security concerns. Embedding journalists with military units allowed for some reporting from the frontlines, albeit under strict supervision. Military spokespersons regularly held press briefings, providing updates and clarifications on the progress of the operation and addressing any concerns raised by media professionals.

Despite these measures, there were instances of alleged censorship and self-censorship, with journalists exercising caution in reporting certain aspects of the operation. This led to a lack of transparency and potentially skewed public perception. Additionally, the limited access to affected communities hindered the media's ability to document the humanitarian challenges and relief efforts during Operation Zarb-e-Azb accurately.

The media coverage and public perception of Operation Zarb-e-Azb in Pakistan were mixed. While some segments of society hailed the military's efforts and saw the operation as a necessary response to the threat of militancy, others criticized the restrictions on reporting and raised concerns about potential human rights violations.

For military historians, understanding the media access and reporting restrictions during Operation Zarb-e-Azb is essential to comprehending the broader context in which the operation unfolded. It highlights the delicate balance between operational security and the need for transparency, as well as the challenges faced by media professionals in reporting on conflicts of this nature.

In conclusion, media access and reporting restrictions during Operation Zarb-e-Azb played a significant role in shaping public perception and understanding of the operation. It is crucial for military historians and those interested in the impact of counter-terrorism efforts to examine the complexities surrounding media coverage during this critical military operation. By doing so, a more comprehensive understanding of Operation Zarb-e-Azb can be achieved.

Propaganda and Psychological Warfare in Media Narratives

In the context of Operation Zarb-e-Azb, the Pakistani military's battle against militant groups in North Waziristan, the role of propaganda and psychological warfare in media narratives cannot be underestimated. This subchapter delves into the various ways in which both the military and the militants strategically use media narratives to shape public perception and advance their respective agendas.

Propaganda serves as a powerful tool for influencing public opinion and rallying support. In the case of Operation Zarb-e-Azb, the Pakistani military carefully crafted a narrative that portrayed the operation as a necessary and decisive action against terrorism. This narrative aimed to garner public support and demonstrate the military's commitment to tackling the menace of militancy. Through press releases, televised speeches, and social media campaigns, the military sought to control the narrative and shape public opinion in favor of the operation.

On the other hand, militant groups also employ propaganda to further their objectives. They exploit media platforms to disseminate their ideology, recruit new members, and instill fear in the local population. By manipulating narratives and using graphic images and videos, they aim to gain sympathy and support for their cause. Moreover, they capitalize on the grievances and dissatisfaction of marginalized communities to garner support and portray themselves as the defenders of the oppressed.

Psychological warfare plays a crucial role in shaping perceptions and manipulating individuals' behavior. Both the military and the militants employ psychological tactics to weaken the enemy's morale and gain an upper hand. For instance, the military may use psychological operations to demoralize militants by disseminating messages of surrender or highlighting the futility of their cause. On the other hand, militants may resort to psychological warfare by spreading fear, rumors, and misinformation to create panic and disrupt normalcy.

The media, as a conduit for information dissemination, plays a vital role in shaping public perception of Operation Zarb-e-Azb. The subchapter examines the media coverage of the operation and its impact on public opinion. It explores the challenges faced by journalists reporting from conflict zones and the ethical considerations involved. Additionally, it delves into the role of social media in shaping narratives and the spread of fake news, highlighting the need for critical media literacy among the public.

By analyzing the role of propaganda and psychological warfare in media narratives during Operation Zarb-e-Azb, military historians gain valuable insights into the complex dynamics of modern warfare. This subchapter serves as a comprehensive exploration of the strategies employed by both the military and militant groups, shedding light on the power of media narratives in shaping public opinion and influencing the outcome of military operations.

Public Opinion and Support for Operation Zarb-e-Azb

One of the key factors in the success of any military operation is the support and approval it receives from the public. Operation Zarb-e-Azb, the Pakistani military's battle against militant groups in North Waziristan, was no exception. Understanding public opinion and support for this operation is crucial in analyzing its impact and effectiveness.

Public opinion in Pakistan regarding Operation Zarb-e-Azb was largely positive. The people of Pakistan had long suffered from the devastating effects of terrorism and militancy. The operation aimed to eliminate these threats and restore peace and stability in the region. As a result, the public viewed it as a necessary and justifiable action.

The devastating terrorist attack on an army-run school in Peshawar in December 2014 further galvanized public support for the operation. The brutal attack, which claimed the lives of over 130 children, shocked the nation and created a sense of urgency to eradicate terrorism. The military's swift response and the initiation of Operation Zarb-e-Azb received widespread approval from the public.

The media played a significant role in shaping public opinion during the operation. The extensive coverage of military operations and the sacrifices made by the armed forces created a sense of pride and nationalism among the people. The media highlighted the successes of the operation, such as the elimination of key militant leaders and the dismantling of their networks, further bolstering public support.

Additionally, the government's efforts to provide humanitarian assistance and relief to the affected communities also played a crucial role in garnering public support. The military worked in collaboration with various relief organizations to provide food, shelter, and medical aid to those displaced by the operation. These efforts were widely appreciated by the public and helped strengthen their trust in the operation.

Overall, public opinion and support for Operation Zarb-e-Azb were instrumental in its success. The people of Pakistan recognized the importance of eliminating militant groups and restoring peace in the region. The media's coverage and the government's relief efforts further contributed to the positive perception of the operation. Understanding the impact of public opinion on military operations is vital for future counter-terrorism efforts, as it can help in garnering support and building a united front against terrorism.

Media's Role in Shaping National Security Discourse and Perception

The media plays a crucial role in shaping national security discourse and perception, especially in the context of military operations such as Operation Zarb-e-Azb. As military historians, it is important to understand the influence and impact of media coverage on the public's perception of these operations and their significance in counter-terrorism efforts.

Operation Zarb-e-Azb, the 2014-2017 Pakistani military operation against militant groups in North Waziristan, received extensive coverage from both local and international media outlets. The media's role in shaping national security discourse during this operation cannot be understated. Through their reporting, media organizations had the power to influence public opinion, create narratives, and shape the overall perception of the operation.

One of the key aspects of the media's role was its ability to highlight the successes and effectiveness of Operation Zarb-e-Azb in eliminating militant groups. By showcasing the military's achievements and highlighting the dismantling of militant networks, the media played a crucial role in boosting public confidence in the operation and the military's ability to counter terrorism.

However, media coverage was not without its challenges. The media faced the difficult task of navigating the fine line between providing accurate information and maintaining national security. Due to the sensitive nature of counter-terrorism operations, certain details had to be withheld to protect ongoing military efforts. This presented a challenge for media organizations, as they had to strike a balance between informing the public and respecting operational security concerns.

Another important aspect to consider is the media's impact on regional security dynamics. Media coverage of Operation Zarb-e-Azb had the potential to shape perceptions not only within Pakistan but also among neighboring countries. The portrayal of the operation could have influenced regional actors' perspectives on Pakistan's commitment to combating terrorism, potentially impacting cooperation and collaboration in future counter-terrorism efforts.

In conclusion, the media's role in shaping national security discourse and perception during Operation Zarb-e-Azb was significant. As military historians, it is essential to analyze media coverage and its impact on public opinion, regional dynamics, and the success and effectiveness of counter-terrorism operations. We must recognize the power and responsibility of the media in shaping national security narratives and work towards a greater understanding of these dynamics for future operations.

Chapter 10: The Role of Drone Strikes in Supporting Operation Zarb-e-Azb

Utilization of Armed Drones in Targeted Killings and Surveillance

The utilization of armed drones in targeted killings and surveillance has been a significant aspect of Operation Zarb-e-Azb, the Pakistani military's battle against militant groups in North Waziristan. This subchapter aims to shed light on the role of armed drones in supporting the operation and its implications for military historians.

Armed drones, also known as unmanned aerial vehicles (UAVs), have played a crucial role in Operation Zarb-e-Azb by providing real-time intelligence, surveillance, and reconnaissance capabilities. These drones have been instrumental in identifying high-value targets and gathering critical information about the movements and activities of militant groups in the region.

The use of armed drones in targeted killings has allowed the Pakistani military to neutralize key militant leaders and disrupt their operational capabilities. By targeting specific individuals with precision strikes, armed drones have significantly degraded the leadership and command structure of militant groups in North Waziristan.

Furthermore, armed drones have been effective in conducting surveillance and monitoring the border regions, aiding in preventing the infiltration of militants and securing the volatile areas. Their ability to cover vast territories and provide persistent surveillance has been crucial in detecting and countering the threat posed by militant groups.

However, the utilization of armed drones in targeted killings and surveillance has not been without controversy. Critics argue that the use of armed drones raises legal and ethical concerns, particularly regarding civilian casualties and the violation of national sovereignty.

Military historians will find this subchapter valuable in understanding the strategic advantages and challenges associated with the use of armed drones in counter-terrorism operations. It provides insights into the evolving nature of modern warfare, where advanced technology plays a pivotal role in shaping military strategies and tactics.

By examining the utilization of armed drones in Operation Zarb-e-Azb, military historians can gain a deeper understanding of how these unmanned systems have revolutionized the concept of warfare and influenced future counter-terrorism operations. They can also analyze the effectiveness of armed drones in eliminating militant groups, the ethical implications of their use, and the impact they have on regional security dynamics.

Overall, the subchapter on the utilization of armed drones in targeted killings and surveillance offers a comprehensive analysis of this critical aspect of Operation Zarb-e-Azb, providing military historians with valuable insights into the evolving nature of modern warfare and its implications for future counter-terrorism operations.

Controversies and Legal Implications Surrounding Drone Strikes

Drone strikes have emerged as a significant aspect of modern warfare, particularly in the context of counter-terrorism operations. The use of unmanned aerial vehicles (UAVs) has been both praised and criticized, sparking debates and legal concerns around the world. Operation Zarb-e-Azb, the Pakistani military's battle against militant groups in North Waziristan, was not exempt from these controversies and legal implications surrounding drone strikes.

One of the primary controversies surrounding drone strikes is related to their legality under international law. Critics argue that these strikes violate the sovereignty of the countries in which they occur, as they often target individuals in territories where the United States or other foreign powers do not have official military presence. These concerns raise questions about the legitimacy of such operations and the potential for setting dangerous precedents in terms of violating national sovereignty.

Furthermore, the lack of transparency surrounding drone strikes has also been a point of contention. The secrecy and classified nature of these operations make it difficult to hold those responsible accountable for any potential violations of international law or civilian casualties. The absence of clear guidelines and regulations on the use of drones in armed conflict further complicates the issue and raises ethical concerns.

In addition to legal controversies, drone strikes have faced criticism for their potential to cause civilian casualties. The precision of these strikes is often touted as a significant advantage, but collateral damage remains a grave concern. Reports of innocent civilians being killed or injured in drone strikes have sparked widespread condemnation and fueled anti-American sentiments in the affected regions.

The controversies and legal implications surrounding drone strikes have led to significant debates within the military and among policymakers. Efforts have been made to establish clearer guidelines and regulations to ensure that these operations are conducted within the boundaries of international law. However, achieving a consensus on the use of drones in warfare remains a challenging task.

Military historians studying Operation Zarb-e-Azb and its impact on counter-terrorism efforts in Pakistan must also analyze the controversies and legal implications surrounding drone strikes. Understanding the ethical, legal, and political dimensions of these operations is crucial for comprehending the full scope and consequences of counter-terrorism campaigns. Only through a comprehensive analysis can valuable lessons be learned for future military operations, ultimately contributing to the advancement of international security and counter-terrorism strategies.

Effectiveness and Precision of Drone Strikes in Counter-terrorism Operations

Drone strikes have become a significant component of modern counter-terrorism operations, providing military forces with a unique advantage in targeting and eliminating militant groups. In the context of Operation Zarb-e-Azb, the Pakistani military's battle against militant groups in North Waziristan, the use of drone strikes played a crucial role in achieving the operation's objectives.

Drone strikes have been highly effective in disrupting and dismantling the infrastructure of militant groups operating in North Waziristan. These strikes have targeted key leaders, training camps, and communication networks, severely hampering the capabilities of these organizations. The precision of drone strikes has greatly minimized collateral damage, ensuring that innocent civilians are not caught in the crossfire.

The use of drones has allowed military forces to gather valuable intelligence on militant activities, enabling them to plan and execute targeted operations with precision. Real-time surveillance and reconnaissance provided by these unmanned aerial vehicles have allowed for timely and accurate decision-making, minimizing the risk to military personnel involved in ground operations.

One of the significant advantages of drone strikes is their ability to strike remote and inaccessible areas, where conventional military operations would be challenging or impossible. This has been particularly crucial in North Waziristan, where rugged terrain and the presence of dense forests provided sanctuary to militant groups. The use of drones has effectively neutralized these safe havens, forcing militants to constantly move and disrupting their operational capabilities.

Despite their effectiveness, drone strikes have faced criticism from various quarters, primarily due to concerns over civilian casualties and violations of sovereignty. It is crucial to address these concerns and maintain strict adherence to international law and human rights principles in the use of drones. Civilian casualties should be minimized through continuous refinement of targeting procedures and intelligence gathering.

In conclusion, the use of drone strikes has proven to be a highly effective and precise tool in counter-terrorism operations, as demonstrated during Operation Zarb-e-Azb in North Waziristan. These strikes have significantly disrupted militant groups, dismantled their infrastructure, and provided valuable intelligence. However, it is essential to address the ethical and legal concerns associated with their use to ensure that they are employed responsibly and in accordance with international laws. The lessons learned from Operation Zarb-e-Azb will undoubtedly inform future counter-terrorism operations, highlighting the importance of incorporating drone capabilities into military strategies.

International Perspectives on the Use of Drones in Conflict Zones

In recent years, the use of drones in conflict zones has become a subject of intense debate and scrutiny. This subchapter aims to delve into the international perspectives on the use of drones in the context of Operation Zarb-e-Azb, the Pakistani military's battle against militant groups in North Waziristan from 2014 to 2017.

The use of drones, also known as unmanned aerial vehicles (UAVs), has significantly transformed modern warfare. While some argue that drone strikes have been instrumental in targeting and eliminating high-value targets, others raise concerns regarding their legality, ethics, and potential for collateral damage.

From an international perspective, the use of drones in conflict zones has been a contentious issue. While some countries have embraced this technology and actively employ it in their military operations, others criticize its use as a violation of sovereignty and an infringement on international law.

The United States, for example, has been at the forefront of drone technology and has extensively used it in its counter-terrorism efforts. However, this approach has faced criticism from various quarters, including human rights organizations, who argue that the use of drones often leads to civilian casualties and violates the principles of proportionality and distinction in international humanitarian law.

Other countries, such as Pakistan, have also been affected by the use of drones. The Pakistani government has expressed its concerns over the violation of its sovereignty and the negative impact of drone strikes on civilian populations. These concerns have sparked a broader debate on the effectiveness and legality of drone warfare in the context of counter-terrorism operations.

Moreover, the use of drones in conflict zones raises questions about transparency, accountability, and the potential for abuse. The lack of international consensus on the rules governing the use of drones complicates matters further. The international community must come together to address these concerns and establish clear guidelines and regulations to govern the use of drones in conflict zones.

In conclusion, the use of drones in conflict zones is a complex and controversial issue. This subchapter provides an overview of the international perspectives on this issue, highlighting the differing opinions and concerns surrounding the use of drones in the context of Operation Zarb-e-Azb. It is crucial for military historians and those interested in the impact of counter-terrorism operations to consider these perspectives in order to gain a comprehensive understanding of the challenges and implications associated with the use of drones in conflict zones.

Chapter 11: Lessons Learned from Operation Zarb-e-Azb for Future Counter-terrorism Operations

Key Strategies and Tactics That Proved Successful

In the book "Operation Zarb-e-Azb: Unveiling the Pakistani Military's Battle Against Militant Groups in North Waziristan," it is essential to delve into the key strategies and tactics that proved successful during this significant military operation. This subchapter aims to provide military historians with a comprehensive overview of the strategies and tactics employed by the Pakistani military, which led to the successful execution of Operation Zarb-e-Azb.

One of the key strategies that proved successful was the comprehensive planning and intelligence gathering process. The Pakistani military, in collaboration with various intelligence agencies, meticulously gathered information about the militant groups operating in North Waziristan. This allowed them to identify their hideouts, supply lines, and key leaders, enabling targeted strikes and minimizing collateral damage.

Another crucial strategy was the establishment of strong international collaborations. The Pakistani military recognized the importance of regional and international support in combating terrorism effectively. Through intelligence sharing, joint operations, and training programs, they were able to enhance their capabilities and ensure a coordinated approach to eliminate militant groups in the region.

The effective use of air power and drone strikes played a significant role in the success of Operation Zarb-e-Azb. The Pakistani military utilized its air assets to target militant hideouts and disrupt their communication networks. The integration of drone strikes, conducted in collaboration with the United States, further weakened the militant groups and hindered their ability to regroup.

Furthermore, the Pakistani military employed a strategy of winning hearts and minds by prioritizing humanitarian challenges and relief efforts during the operation. This approach helped build trust and support from the local communities, who had been adversely affected by the presence of these militant groups for years. The provision of food, shelter, and medical aid not only alleviated the suffering of the affected communities but also undermined the support base of the militants.

Lastly, the book highlights the role of intelligence agencies in planning and executing Operation Zarb-e-Azb. These agencies played a critical role in gathering real-time intelligence, conducting surveillance, and identifying potential threats. Their expertise and coordination with the military ensured successful operations and minimized the risk to the security forces.

In conclusion, the success of Operation Zarb-e-Azb can be attributed to a combination of key strategies and tactics employed by the Pakistani military. The comprehensive planning, international collaborations, effective use of air power and drone strikes, humanitarian efforts, and the role of intelligence agencies all played a crucial role in eliminating militant groups from North Waziristan. These lessons learned from Operation Zarb-e-Azb will undoubtedly shape future counter-terrorism operations, not just in Pakistan but also across the globe. Military historians will find this subchapter invaluable in understanding the intricacies and effectiveness of the strategies and tactics employed during this significant military operation.

Challenges and Areas for Improvement in Counter-terrorism Operations

Counter-terrorism operations are complex and multifaceted endeavors that require careful planning, coordination, and execution. Operation Zarb-e-Azb, the Pakistani military's battle against militant groups in North Waziristan, faced several challenges and areas for improvement that can provide valuable insights for military historians and those interested in the operation's impact on counter-terrorism efforts.

One of the significant challenges faced during Operation Zarb-e-Azb was the presence of a vast network of underground tunnels used by militants to hide, store weapons, and conduct their operations. These tunnels provided a safe haven for militants, making it difficult for the military to locate and eliminate them. This challenge highlighted the need for improved intelligence gathering and surveillance techniques to identify and neutralize such hidden infrastructure.

Another area for improvement was the coordination and collaboration between different military and intelligence agencies involved in the operation. Effective communication and information sharing are crucial for the success of any counter-terrorism operation. However, Operation Zarb-e-Azb revealed certain gaps and limitations in this regard, which impacted the overall effectiveness of the operation. Lessons learned from this experience can guide future efforts to enhance inter-agency cooperation.

The humanitarian challenges and relief efforts during Operation Zarb-e-Azb also deserve attention. The massive displacement of civilians and the destruction of infrastructure in the conflict-affected areas posed significant challenges for relief organizations. Coordinating relief efforts, ensuring the provision of essential services, and addressing the psychological and social consequences on affected communities require a comprehensive and integrated approach.

Furthermore, the media coverage and public perception of Operation Zarb-e-Azb played a crucial role in shaping public opinion and support for the operation. The military's efforts to maintain transparency and provide accurate information were essential in countering misinformation and disinformation campaigns. Evaluating the communication strategies employed during the operation can provide valuable insights for future counter-terrorism operations.

Lastly, the impact of drone strikes in supporting Operation Zarb-e-Azb cannot be overlooked. While drones provided valuable intelligence and precision capabilities, their use also raised ethical and legal concerns. Striking a balance between the effectiveness of drone strikes and the protection of civilian lives is an ongoing challenge that requires careful consideration.

In conclusion, Operation Zarb-e-Azb faced several challenges and areas for improvement in counter-terrorism operations. Enhancing intelligence gathering, inter-agency coordination, humanitarian efforts, and communication strategies are crucial for the success of future operations. Furthermore, the ethical and legal implications of using drones in counter-terrorism operations require careful consideration. By analyzing and addressing these challenges, military historians and counter-terrorism experts can contribute to the development of more effective and efficient strategies in the fight against militant groups.

Importance of International Collaboration and Intelligence Sharing

In the complex landscape of counter-terrorism operations, international collaboration and intelligence sharing play a pivotal role in ensuring the success of military campaigns. This subchapter delves into the significance of these factors in the context of Operation Zarb-e-Azb, the Pakistani military's battle against militant groups in North Waziristan from 2014 to 2017.

Operation Zarb-e-Azb marked a turning point in Pakistan's fight against terrorism, and one of the key factors behind its success was the robust international collaboration and intelligence sharing that took place. The operation required a comprehensive understanding of the intricate network of militant groups operating in the region, their transnational links, and their sources of funding and support. This necessitated close coordination between Pakistan's intelligence agencies and their counterparts in other countries.

Intelligence sharing not only allowed for a more comprehensive picture of the threat landscape but also facilitated targeted operations against high-value targets. The exchange of information on known militants, their activities, and their networks enabled the Pakistani military to plan and execute precise strikes, minimizing collateral damage and maximizing the impact on militant groups.

Moreover, international collaboration in terms of logistics, training, and technical support proved crucial during Operation Zarb-e-Azb. The involvement of foreign militaries and intelligence agencies brought in specialized expertise, advanced equipment, and a fresh perspective to the operation. This partnership fostered a multidimensional approach to counter-terrorism efforts, enhancing Pakistan's capacity to combat the evolving threat posed by militant groups.

Furthermore, international collaboration and intelligence sharing extended beyond the military realm, encompassing humanitarian challenges and relief efforts. Humanitarian organizations, both local and international, played a vital role in addressing the needs of the affected communities. The sharing of resources, expertise, and best practices between different actors ensured a more efficient response to the humanitarian crisis resulting from the operation.

In conclusion, the importance of international collaboration and intelligence sharing cannot be overstated in the context of Operation Zarb-e-Azb. These factors enabled a comprehensive understanding of the threat landscape, facilitated targeted operations, enhanced the provides valuable insights for military historians and those interested in understanding the complexities of counter-terrorism operations. By analyzing the various aspects of this operation, policymakers, military strategists, and scholars can derive valuable lessons to inform future counter-terrorism endeavors.